It's My State!

NEW HAMPSHIRE

The Granite State

Kerry Jones Waring, Terry Allan Hicks, and William McGeveran

Cavendish Square

New York

3 9082 13140 3092

Published in 2016 by Cavendish Square Publishing, LLC
243 5th Avenue, Suite 136, New York, NY 10016

Library of Congress Cataloging-in-Publication Data

Waring, Kerry Jones.
New Hampshire / Kerry Jones Waring, Terry Allan Hicks, and William McGeveran.
pages cm
Includes bibliographical references and index.
ISBN 978-1-62713-166-7 (hardcover) ISBN 978-1-62713-168-1 (ebook)
1. New Hampshire—Juvenile literature. I. Hicks, Terry Allan. II. McGeveran, William. III. Title.

F34.3.W37 2015
974.2—dc23

2015000577

Editorial Director: David McNamara
Editor: Fletcher Doyle
Copy Editor: Rebecca Rohan
Art Director: Jeffrey Talbot
Designer: Joseph Macri
Senior Production Manager: Jennifer Ryder-Talbot
Production Editor: Renni Johnson
Photo Research: J8 Media

The photographs in this book are used by permission and through the courtesy of: Lee Snider Photo Images/Shutterstock.com, cover; Age Fotostock/Superstock, 4; Steve Byland/Shutterstock.com, 4; Age Fotostock/Superstock, 4; Steve Oehlenschlager/Shutterstock.com, 5; Dgmata/Shutterstock.com, 5; Corbis Flirt/Alamy, 5; Tetra Images/Alamy, 6; The Pilot's-Eye View/Shutterstock.com, 7; EcoPhotography.com/ Alamy, 9; Westgraphix LLC, 10; Saugus Photos Online/Alamy, 11; Erin Paul Donovan/Superstock, 12; Garry Black/Alamy, 13; Jeffrey M. Frank/Shutterstock.com, 14; Donald R. Swartz/ Shutterstock.com, 14; Erin Paul Donovan/Alamy, 14; MdN/Shutterstock.com, 15; Linda Cendes/File:SquamLake.JPG/Wikimedia Commons, 15; Phil Schermeister/Corbis, 16; NHPA/Superstock, 17; Erin Paul Donovan/Superstock, 18; Kevin Schafer/Alamy, 24; Cornforth Images/Alamy, 20; All Canada Photos/Superstock, 20; MariaBrzostowska/iStock/Thinkstock, 20; Jason Patrick Ross/Shutterstock.com, 21; Hemera Technologies/Photos.com/Thinkstock, 21; National Geographic/Getty Images, 21; Stock Montage/Getty Images, 22; Washington Imaging/Alamy, 24; Edward Fielding/Shutterstock.com, 27; North Wind Picture Archives/Alamy, 28; North Wind Picture Archives/Alamy, 29; Doug Menuez/Stockbyte/Getty Images, 30; Keystone/Stringer/Getty Images, 33; Jeffrey M. Frank/Shutterstock.com, 34; AlexiusHoratius/File:Downtown Dover51.JPG/Wikimedia Commons, 34; Rklawton/File:City Hall & Opera House, Rochester, NH 2013. JPG/Wikimedia Commons, 35; Robert Estall photo agency/Alamy, 35; Corbis, 36; Philip Scalia/Alamy, 37; National Archives, 38; Visions of America/Superstock, 39; Universal Images Group Limited/Alamy, 40; Philip Scalia/Alamy, 41; Pat Canova/Photolibrary/Getty Images, 44; North Wind Picture Archives/Alamy, 46; Featureflash/Shutterstock.com, 48; Brooks Kraft/Corbis, 48; Helga Esteb/Shutterstock.com, 48; PCN Photography/Alamy, 49; Michael Tran/FilmMagic, 49; Chip Somodevilla/Getty Images, 49; Accurate Art, 50; Greg Ryan/Alamy, 51; Ian Bradley/Alamy, 52; Strawbery Banke Museum, 54; Philip Scalia/Alamy, 54; Vespasian/Alamy, 55; Courtesy Monadnock Film Festival 55; Jonathan Wiggs/The Boston Globe via Getty Images,56; Sandy Macys/Alamy, 58; Kevin Shields/Alamy, 60; Erin Paul Donovan/Alamy, 61; North Wind Picture Archives/Alamy, 62; Everett Historical/Shutterstock.com, 62; Darren McCollester/Getty Images,62; Marc Nozell/File:Governor John Lynch.jpg/Wikimedia Commons, 63; Age Fotostock/Superstock, 64; AP Photo/Lee Marriner, 67; Bob Shirtz/Superstock, 68; Len Rubenstein/Superstock, 68; Philip Scalia/Alamy, 69; Stuart Kelly/Alamy, 69; Robyn Mackenzie/Shutterstock.com, 70; Nordic Photos/Superstock, 72; Christopher Santoro, 74; Hemis/Alamy, 75; AlexiusHoratius/File:Keene NH 26.JPG/Wikimedia Commons, 75; Christopher Santoro (2), 76.

Printed in the United States of America

NEW HAMPSHIRE
CONTENTS

A Quick Look at New Hampshire 4

1. The Granite State 7
New Hampshire County Map 10
New Hampshire Population by County 11
10 Key Sites 14
10 Key Plants and Animals 20

2. From the Beginning 23
The Native People 26
Making a Cornhusk Doll 30
10 Key Cities 34
10 Key Dates 43

3. The People 45
10 Key People 48
10 Key Events 54

4. How the Government Works 57
Political Figures from New Hampshire 62
You Can Make a Difference 63

5. Making a Living 65
10 Key Industries 68
Recipe for Garlic Lemon Shrimp 70

New Hampshire State Map 74
New Hampshire Map Skills 75
State Flag, Seal, and Song 76
Glossary 77
More About New Hampshire 78
Index 79

★ State Tree: White Birch

This tall, graceful tree is sometimes called the canoe birch, because Native Americans made fast, lightweight canoes from its bark. It can grow to be eighty feet tall. New Hampshire's early settlers commonly used birch bark to write on, since paper was expensive. The white birch became New Hampshire's state tree in 1947.

★ State Bird: Purple Finch

The purple finch is a favorite with the state's farmers and gardeners, because it eats insects that can harm crops and other plants. The male bird, with its purplish color, has been described as a "sparrow dipped in raspberry juice." The purple finch is also known for its distinct musical warble, or song.

★ State Flower: Purple Lilac

Benning Wentworth, who in the mid-1700s was the first colonial governor of New Hampshire, imported these showy flowers from England and planted them in his garden. The lilac's big, sweet-smelling blossoms are welcome signs of spring in New Hampshire. Lilac bushes can live for hundreds of years.

NEW HAMPSHIRE

POPULATION: 1,316,470

★ State Animal: White-Tailed Deer

New Hampshire's state animal is named for its white-edged tail. The deer raises its tail when it feels threatened, to alert other deer to possible danger. Once overhunted, these deer have become common. They are often found even in urban and suburban areas and unfortunately can cause accidents on the road.

★ State Rock: Granite

Granite quarrying (taking granite from the ground) was once an important New Hampshire industry. In fact, "the Granite State" is one of New Hampshire's nicknames. The Washington Monument, parts of New York's Brooklyn Bridge, and the cornerstone of the United Nations building are all made of New Hampshire granite.

★ State Dog: Chinook

In 2009, seventh-grade students from Bedford got the legislature to name the Chinook as the official state dog. This rare breed was developed in New Hampshire by an explorer named Arthur Treadwell Walden. Chinooks were often used as sled dogs. They are affectionate and playful animals, and good family pets.

The Portsmouth Harbor Light, built on the site of a light station put up in 1771, is a working lighthouse.

The Granite State

New Hampshire gets its nickname, the Granite State, from the granite mining industry that once flourished there. The nickname also brings to mind the state's rugged people and their spirit of independence. In fact, New Hampshirites set up their own government and declared independence from Great Britain in January 1776, six months before representatives of all thirteen British colonies along the Atlantic Coast joined to adopt the Declaration of Independence.

Today, residents and visitors alike enjoy the state's scenic mountains, lakes, and woodland trails, both in summer, when the weather is warm, and during winter, when snow blankets the ground to the delight of skiers, skaters, and snowboarders. Every four years, in the midst of winter, ambitious politicians descend upon the state to meet and greet New Hampshirites, listen to their concerns, and seek their votes in the New Hampshire presidential primary, the first **primary election** in the contest for the White House.

With a total area of 9,350 square miles (24,216 square kilometers), New Hampshire is the fifth-smallest state in the country. It is a little smaller than its neighbor Vermont, but it is bigger than New Jersey, Connecticut, Delaware, and Rhode Island. Much of the landscape was formed thousands of years ago by retreating glaciers (large slow-moving masses of ice) and a harsh climate. Over time, wind and water gradually helped to shape the state's features.

New Hampshire can be divided into three main regions. They are the Coastal Lowlands, the Eastern New England Upland, and the White Mountains. New Hampshire has ten counties. The biggest county by population is Hillsborough, in the south, where about 30 percent of the people live. Coos County, in the far north, is the largest by land area but smallest by population. Many New Englanders spend their vacations in the White Mountains, which cover much of Coos County and parts of Grafton and Carroll counties.

The Coastal Lowlands

New Hampshire has barely 18 miles (29 kilometers) of seacoast, in its southeast corner where the Piscataqua River meets the Atlantic Ocean. Europeans first settled in the Coastal Lowlands. One of the towns they built, Strawbery Banke (now called Portsmouth), grew into a major shipbuilding center and served as New Hampshire's first capital.

Portsmouth is still a working seaport, and the seacoast is now an important tourist destination. Among the region's best-known attractions are the Isles of Shoals, about 6 miles (10 km) out in Piscataqua Bay. Captain John Smith was the first English settler to map the Isles of Shoals. These beautiful islands feature a famous garden created by Celia Thaxter, who lived there and in the nineteenth century was well known as a poet. Also on the islands is a research laboratory that studies life in the surrounding waters.

The Eastern New England Upland

The Eastern New England Upland takes up most of southern New Hampshire and about half the state overall. Most of New Hampshire's major cities and towns—including Manchester, Nashua, and the state capital, Concord—are found in the river valleys of the Upland. In the early 1900s, factories and mills began to appear here, powered by the fast-moving Merrimack River.

Most of the state's once-famous granite quarries are found in the Upland, especially around Concord. The area also has many fruit and dairy farms. New Hampshire has around 1,300 lakes or ponds. The Upland is home to the largest of these lakes, Lake Winnipesaukee, which covers almost 80 square miles (a little more than 200 sq km). It is a popular vacation spot, especially in the summertime.

The most unusual sights in the New Hampshire landscape may be the Monadnocks. These tall, isolated hills made of rock were too

New Hampshire Borders	
North:	Canada
South:	Massachusetts
East:	Maine
	Atlantic Ocean
West:	Vermont

Mount Monadnock draws more hikers than any other mountain in North America.

hard to be worn down by the moving glaciers. The highest, Mount Monadnock, has been a favorite of hikers since the nineteenth century. It is said that about 125,000 people each year finish the 3,165-foot (965-meter) climb to its peak, making it the most climbed mountain in North America.

The White Mountains

The White Mountains are named for their chalk peaks, which shine a brilliant white, even during the summer months. They take up the northern third of New Hampshire. The dense forests that cover the mountainsides supply lumber for construction and wood pulp for paper. The steep mountain valleys in this region are called notches. Tourists come here year-round. In the summer, the mountains are ideal for hiking and white-water rafting and kayaking. In the winter, skiers and snowboarders enjoy the deep, powdery snow.

The best-known section of the White Mountains is the Presidential Range. Its six highest peaks, named for former presidents or other American statesmen, are all more

NEW ★ HAMPSHIRE
COUNTY MAP

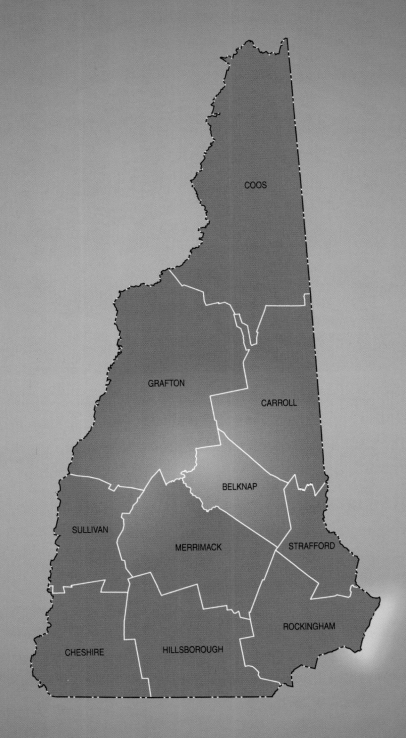

COOS

GRAFTON

CARROLL

BELKNAP

SULLIVAN

MERRIMACK

STRAFFORD

ROCKINGHAM

CHESHIRE

HILLSBOROUGH

NEW HAMPSHIRE

POPULATION BY COUNTY

Belknap	60,088
Carroll	47,818
Cheshire	77,117
Coos	33,055
Grafton	89,118
Hillsborough	400,721
Merrimack	146,445
Rockingham	295,223
Strafford	123,143
Sullivan	43,742

Source: US Bureau of the Census, 2010

Spectacular Franconia Notch State Park is in Grafton County.

The Mount Washington Cog Railway climbs the tallest mountain in the northeast.

than a mile (1,600 m) high. The 6,288-foot (1,916 m) Mount Washington is the tallest mountain in the northeastern United States. Visitors come here in warm weather to ride the little steam-powered trains of the Mount Washington Cog Railway. Trains have been chugging up and down the steep mountainside since 1869. The mountain has an average grade of 25 percent, and the train is the second steepest rack railway (a cog fits into a ladder-like rack to help the train climb) in the world.

Visitors can drive to the top of Mount Washington. Workers completed what is now the Mount Washington Auto Road in 1861. They had to drill blasting holes in the rock by hand, use black powder (dynamite had not yet been discovered), and move countless tons of rock and gravel. They spent the nights in tents on the mountainside, often braving snow, frigid temperatures, and high winds. Today, it takes about two hours to complete the drive up the mountain. The weather on the top of Mount Washington is known for changing quickly, with frequent hurricane-force winds and plenty of **precipitation**, meaning rain or snow. Those who work in the Mount Washington Observatory have dubbed it "Home of the World's Worst Weather." Mount Washington is also the subject of many paintings, thanks to an art movement in the early twentieth century called "White Mountain art," during which many painters visited the region to create new works.

But it was farther north, in the Franconia Range, where nature created New Hampshire's most beloved symbol: the world-famous Old Man of the Mountain. This jagged rock formation was carved into the side of Cannon Mountain (also called Profile Mountain), near Franconia Notch, by centuries of wind, rain, and snow. It looked a lot like the face of a proud, tough old man.

Imagine how shocked the people of New Hampshire were on May 3, 2003, when they discovered that the Old Man of the Mountain was gone. The rocks that made up the famous face had fallen to the valley below, worn down by harsh weather and shaken by road traffic in the vicinity. In 2010, work began on a memorial to the famous landmark. The profile plaza, which includes seven steel profilers that recreate the stone face, was dedicated in June 2011.

The iconic **Old Man of the Mountain** rock formation before it fell in 2003.

10 KEY SITES ★ ★ ★

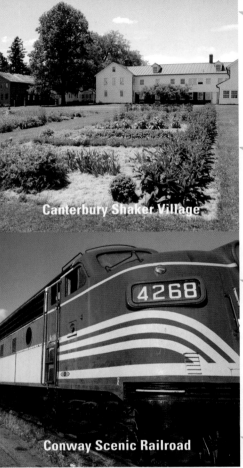

Canterbury Shaker Village

Conway Scenic Railroad

Franconia Notch State Park

1. Canterbury Shaker Village

The Shakers believe in simple living, equality, and community. This museum in Canterbury preserves a two hundred-year-old Shaker village, including thirty buildings and 694 acres of forest, to give visitors a sense of what life was like in this community.

2. Castle in the Clouds

Moultonborough is home to this mountaintop estate built between 1913 and 1914. The castle follows an architectural style known as Arts and Crafts, a movement that teaches that structures should be built in harmony with surrounding nature.

3. Conway Scenic Railroad

In 1974, the Boston & Maine railroad station in North Conway Village was restored, offering visitors the chance to experience the "golden age of railroading." Vintage passenger cars take riders through historic routes to nearby towns Conway and Bartlett.

4. Currier Museum of Art

The Currier Museum of Art in Manchester is internationally renowned. Visitors can view European and American paintings, decorative arts, photographs and sculpture, by artists including Pablo Picasso, Claude Monet, and Georgia O'Keeffe. Children and adults can take classes here.

5. Franconia Notch State Park

New Hampshire is known for its natural beauty, and Franconia Notch State Park is among its most beautiful areas. The park's noted features include Flume Gorge, Cannon Mountain, and the New England Ski Museum.

6. Lost River Gorge and Boulder Caves

Massive glaciers once moved across North America, carving rock formations like New Hampshire's Lost River Gorge and Boulder Caves. Visitors can take hikes and walks through the area, or enjoy special events such as nighttime tours.

7. Mount Washington

Tourists may drive their cars up the eight-mile trail to the summit of Mount Washington. In the winter, visitors can take the Mount Washington SnowCoach, an all-terrain vehicle that offers safe tours through the snow.

8. Santa's Village

It's Christmas all year at Santa's Village in Jefferson. In spite of its holiday theme, the park is popular in summer and fall. Features include the Ho Ho H2O Water Park, Reindeer Carousel, and a Skyway Sleigh that provides great views of the park.

9. Squam Lakes Natural Science Center

Visitors can learn about nature through experience at this center in Holderness. Exhibits offer a look at the habitats of animals including coyotes, deer, mountain lions, owls, and more. A wetlands walk and geology exhibit are also included.

10. USS *Albacore*

This US Navy submarine, now located in Portsmouth, once broke the world record for submarine speed by going 40 miles per hour (64.4 kmh) underwater. Today, Albacore Park gives visitors the chance to view the submarine on land and learn about its history at sea.

Lost River Gorge and Boulder Caves

Squam Lake

USS *Albacore*

New Hampshire is sometimes called "the Mother of Rivers" because five of New England's great rivers begin there: the Androscoggin, Connecticut, Merrimack, Piscataqua, and Saco. In all, the state has more than 40,000 miles (65,000 km) of rivers.

The Climate

Winter in New Hampshire is not for everybody. The weather varies by region and altitude, but it is reliably cold. High up in the White Mountains, on Mount Washington, daily low temperatures in January average about −4 degrees Fahrenheit (−20 degrees Celsius). In the city of Concord, in the Upland region to the south, daily low temperatures in January average about 10°F (−12°C). There is plenty of snow, too. Concord gets an average of 64 inches (163 centimeters) a year.

Mount Washington gets an average of around 260 inches (660 centimeters) of snow each winter. The weather observatory at the top of the mountain has often seen unusual weather conditions. The observatory registered what stood for many years as the highest surface wind speed ever recorded—231 miles (372 km) per hour—on April 12, 1934. In 2010, however, meteorologists concluded that this wind speed was exceeded at least once, in April 1996, when the wind speed reached 253 miles (408 km) per hour during a cyclone on an offshore island in Western Australia.

Winter often puts the Mount Washington weather observatory in its icy grip.

While some New Hampshirites enjoy the state's cold, snowy winters, others learn to bear them. As one resident has said, "The best thing about a New Hampshire winter is the way it makes you appreciate a New Hampshire spring." In fact, there is much to enjoy on a bright spring day when the weather is warming, the purple lilacs are in bloom, and the many apple and cherry trees show off their blossoms. But spring days in New Hampshire can often be rainy, and even when the sun is out, melting snow often creates a great deal of mud. Locals also know that spring is black fly season in New Hampshire. These pests usually emerge in May and stick around until June. They are most common near bodies of water, but with the state's abundant lakes and streams, few New Hampshirites are spared.

New Hampshire is at its finest in the fall.

Summers are generally pleasant. Occasionally, the weather gets very hot. On the Fourth of July in 1911, the temperature in Nashua reached 106°F (41°C), setting a record for the state. Humidity can also be a problem. But most days are sunny and warm. July temperatures in Concord average about 70°F (21°C).

For many people, New Hampshire is at its best in the fall, when the trees of this heavily wooded state blaze with brilliant red, gold, and yellow leaves. "Leaf peepers" come to New Hampshire in autumn to enjoy the stunning scenery and crisp weather. On October days in Concord, the average high temperature is still around 60°F (16°C), but blankets are needed on autumn nights, when temperatures typically drop to just above freezing.

Pumpkinpalooza

Each fall, the Keene Pumpkin Festival tries to bring the world's greatest number of jack-o'-lanterns to one spot. In 2014, there were 21,912 carved pumpkins counted at the festival. Keene has a population of nearly twenty-three thousand, and more than double that number of visitors usually attend the festival.

Life in the Wild

New Hampshire is home to a dazzling variety of wildlife, both plants and animals. Forests cover about 84 percent of the state—a bigger proportion than in any other state except Maine. The trees in the northern part of New Hampshire are mostly evergreens, such as fir and spruce. In the central and southern parts of the state, the forests are mixed and may include white pine, maple, oak, and white birch, New Hampshire's state tree.

When spring comes, hundreds of species of wildflowers begin to appear, including trillium, pink lady's slippers, asters, buttercups, and blue, yellow, and white violets. Wild shrubs, such as mountain laurel and blueberry bushes, grow in the state, too.

Black bears, white-tailed deer, elk, and moose can be found all over the state, and there are less-common animals such as the marten and the Canadian lynx. Many New Hampshire residents have heard the mournful calls of coyotes at night, especially in the spring and fall when they are the most vocal. Game birds such as grouse, wild turkeys, and woodcocks also make their home in New Hampshire.

The mountain ponds of northern New Hampshire are filled with brook trout. The lakes in the center of the state have many other species of trout, as well as certain types of salmon and smallmouth bass. The waters off the seacoast are also rich with life. Striped bass and bluefish are common. Marine mammals such as dolphins, porpoises, and whales also live in the coastal waters.

Progress has been made in maintaining the populations of many animal species, but the news for wildlife in New Hampshire is not all good. As land is developed for other uses, there is less room

The variety of wildlife in New Hampshire includes the majestic moose.

for certain types of plants and animals. Air pollution, often from other states or from Canada, is also a problem, and harmful substances can get into rivers and streams and enter the ground. New Hampshire's government and businesses have taken many steps to help control and prevent pollution of the air, ground and water. The New Hampshire Department of Environmental Services began a Pollution Prevention Program that helps manufacturers and other businesses. The program offers free monitoring and evaluation of facilities to ensure they are operating as cleanly and efficiently as possible.

The Canadian lynx is easily identified by the tufts of black fur on the tips of its ears.

A few animal species, including the gray wolf, Canadian lynx, timber rattlesnake, Karner blue butterfly, and piping plover, are on the state's endangered species list. This means they are in danger of becoming extinct (completely gone) in the state. In addition, American marten, spotted turtle, and common loon are among species listed as threatened. This means they could become endangered if conditions do not improve. Scientists and concerned residents continue to work together to help protect the state's wildlife.

In 1997, New Hampshire Fish and Game's Nongame and Endangered Wildlife Program began an effort to revive the piping plover population in the state. Beginning in the 1940s, these birds had been steadily disappearing due to loss of and damage to their habitat, as well as human disturbances. By the 1990s, it was thought that the plover was entirely gone, until a jogger found one nesting on the beach in 1996. Since then, the state has started efforts that include protecting areas where piping plovers build their nests, keeping beaches safe and clean for the birds, and even having a "plover monitor" who keeps track of the piping plover population and educates beachgoers. Residents can also volunteer to help monitor the nests and chicks of these birds. By 2013, 218 piping plover chicks had been hatched in New Hampshire.

Bald Eagle

Beaver

Box Elder

1. Bald Eagle

In 1989, these magnificent birds of prey were seen nesting in New Hampshire for the first time in forty years. In recent years, bald eagles have returned in increasing numbers. They are now listed as threatened instead of endangered.

2. Beaver

These hardworking, intelligent animals live in groups in lodges. Beavers build dams that block rivers and ponds. The dams create wetlands, but they can also cause floods. Beavers were once endangered in New Hampshire, but by the 1950s their numbers had increased.

3. Black Bear

The shy black bear prefers deep woods with few humans nearby. An adult male usually weighs 200–250 pounds (90–115 kilograms). There are believed to be more than five thousand black bears in the state.

4. Box Elder

The box elder grows often on the banks of streams or rivers, but can also be found in urban settings. While box elder's soft wood cannot be used to make things, it does help stabilize the riverbanks on which it grows.

5. Little Brown Bat

These mammals live in barns, attics, and similar places in warm weather, and hibernate in old mines. They can eat half their body weight in insects each night. Like other bats, they find their way by **echolocation**.

NEW HAMPSHIRE

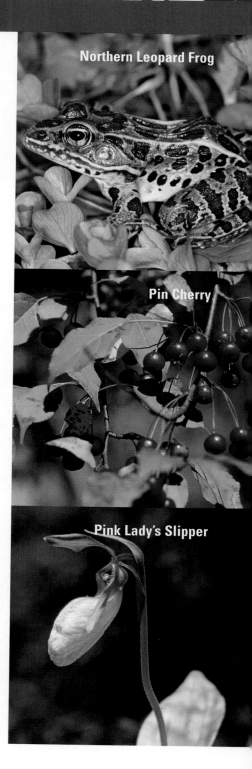

Northern Leopard Frog

Pin Cherry

Pink Lady's Slipper

6. Lupine

The wild lupine grows best along highways and in other open areas. Forest fires create good habitats for it by burning tree canopy and allowing sunlight to reach the plants. As fire prevention improves, lupines have become less common in the state.

7. Northern Leopard Frog

This frog, recognizable by its green skin and brown spots, can be found in ponds, marshes, and slow streams in New Hampshire. The frog's population has been dwindling due to **habitat loss** and pollution.

8. Pin Cherry

The pin cherry has a straight trunk and rounded crown, or top. Clusters of white flowers and small, sour cherries grow on the pin cherry. This small tree often grows in dry, open clearings after forest fires.

9. Pink Lady's Slipper

This delicate wild orchid—New Hampshire's official wildflower—is sometimes called the moccasin flower. Pink lady's slipper grows in shady forests and takes a long time to mature. Its leaves fold over to hide a single blossom that looks like a little shoe.

10. Red Osier Dogwood

The red osier dogwood is a hardy shrub. Its red leaves make it a popular plant for decorating gardens. The plant has a strong root system that helps prevent **soil erosion**, which happens when wind or rain moves soil away.

Captain John Smith gave the region that now includes New Hampshire the name New England.

From the Beginning

People have lived in what is now New Hampshire since shortly after the glaciers melted, more than ten thousand years ago. Archaeologists have found remains of stone tools dating back to around that time. Scientists believe the earliest inhabitants were nomadic, living mostly in wetlands or near rivers, lakes, and streams. The town of Salem, in the southeast, is home to "Mystery Hill"—which has also been dubbed "America's Stonehenge." Some people believe that this now-ruined maze of stone walls and chambers could have been built by ancient people, perhaps by explorers from northern Europe, some four thousand years ago and used as a solar calendar to mark the passing seasons. Others believe it was put together by New England farmers in more recent times. Nobody knows for sure.

Because of the region's challenging climate and short growing season, it is thought that its first residents relied heavily on hunting. They hunted game such as deer, moose, and bear. They also fished and ate wild plants. Later inhabitants learned to farm despite the challenges of the land and climate. They raised crops of corn, beans, and squash. This farming made it possible for people to settle into small permanent communities.

By the early seventeenth century, when the first European settlers arrived from England, the New Hampshire area may have been home to about five thousand

Native Americans. They belonged mostly to the Western Abenaki nation, which included a number of Algonquian-speaking groups. The region's Native American tribes—the Piscataqua, Nashua, Pennacook, Coosuc, and Ossipee—usually lived in peace with one another. They did, however, sometimes go to war against the Iroquois, who lived to the north and west. Contact with European settlers, who were drawn to the resources of the area, put many new pressures on the Native Americans.

The Europeans

The first visitors to the area from Europe may have been Vikings. These sailors from Scandinavia (a part of northern Europe) began exploring North America's northern Atlantic Coast around the tenth century, and some seem to have reached a part of what is now New Hampshire. Markings on a rock near the town of Hampton may be runes (Viking writing) that were carved around 1100 CE. But if the Vikings did reach this region, they did not stay for long.

The Strawbery Banke Museum gives visitors a taste of colonial life.

During the 1500s and early 1600s, Giovanni da Verrazzano and, later, Samuel de Champlain (both exploring for France) sailed along the seacoast of what is now New Hampshire. But it was the English sea cavptain John Smith who first brought the area to the attention of Europe. Smith is famous for founding Jamestown, Virginia, the first permanent English colony in North America, in 1607. But on a later voyage, in 1614, he sailed to the coast of what he named "New England" and visited the Isles of Shoals and the nearby seacoast.

In 1622, the English king gave a huge piece of land in New England to Captain John Mason and Sir Ferdinando Gorges. Seven years later, the two men divided it between them. Mason took the section between the Merrimack and Piscataqua Rivers and named it New Hampshire, after his home county of Hampshire in England. Gorges's section eventually became the state of Maine.

Settlers began arriving in the area at the mouth of the Piscataqua in the early 1620s. A small group built Pannaway Plantation, at Odiorne's Point, near the present-day town of Rye. Around 1630, another group settled at a place they called Strawbery Banke. The settlement was named for the wild berries that grew there. Years later, the town would become known as Portsmouth.

These settlers came in search of fish to catch, land to farm, and trees to cut. They built salt works for preserving fish and saw mills to cut lumber for houses and ships. They also occupied land where the Native Americans hunted and fished and brought diseases to which the Native Americans had no resistance. Eventually up to three-quarters or more of the Native American population died from these diseases alone. Relations between settlers and the Native tribes were strained, but open warfare was avoided for a time.

War and Revolution

Beginning in the late seventeenth century, England fought a long series of wars with its biggest rival, France, for control of the eastern part of North America. Many Native American tribes joined in the fighting, most of them siding with the French, with whom they had better relations. New Hampshire became directly involved in June 1689. A group of Native Americans—angry especially because hundreds of their people had been captured and killed or sold into slavery—killed twenty-three settlers in the town of Dover. They also captured others and sold them as slaves to the French.

Many New Hampshire soldiers eventually joined in battles against the French, including five hundred men who helped capture the French fortress at Louisbourg, in present-day Nova Scotia, in 1758. The last in this series of wars, commonly called the

The Native People

Native American tribes lived in the area that would become New Hampshire for many thousands of years before the arrival of European settlers. The two main tribes that resided there were the Abenaki and Pennacook people. These tribes were closely related. Some historians consider the Pennacook to be part of the Abenaki. The Abenaki people lived in the northern part of the state, and the Pennacook lived mostly in the south. Both the Abenaki and Pennacook spoke variations of an Algonquian-based language, with each having its own dialect.

The Abenaki and Pennacook had very similar cultures and ways of life, especially before the arrival of European settlers. Both tribes relied on agriculture as a main food source, raising corn, beans, and squash. Many lived near rivers or other bodies of water, as the soil was most fertile there. The Abenaki and Pennacook also hunted animals like moose, deer, rabbit, and turkey, using the game they caught for food, clothing and shelter. They fished and gathered wild berries. Some made maple syrup from tree sap.

The arrival of European settlers changed the lives of many Abenaki and Pennacook. Many of the Native people caught diseases from the Europeans that they had never had before, and to which they had no resistance. A large number of Abenaki and Pennacook became sick and died from these illnesses. Many others were driven from their land by the Europeans. Displacement and war with the settlers and other tribes forced most of the members of both tribes to move north to Quebec and other neighboring regions.

Today, there are no federally recognized tribes in New Hampshire. That means there are no reservations or official governments for Native Americans in the state. Most of the Pennacook people moved to other places and merged with other tribes, including the Abenaki. The population of Abenaki in New Hampshire is still small, but has grown slowly in recent decades. The remaining population continues to take pride in its culture and history by sharing it with fellow New Hampshire residents through festivals and art.

Spotlight on the Abenaki

The word Abenaki means "people of the east" or "people of the dawnlands." Abenaki people also sometimes call themselves Alnombak, which means "the people."

Clans and Groups: The Abenaki are organized into clans based around families. The Abenaki tribe, together with the Maliseet, Passamaquoddy, Mi'kmaq, and Penobscot Indians, were members of a group called the Wabanaki Confederacy.

The Abenaki and the Pennacook both built wigwams using birch bark.

Homes: The Abenaki lived in small buildings made with the bark of birch trees called **wigwams** or lodges. Others preferred to live in larger structures called **longhouses**, a kind of home that is most often associated with the Iroquois.

Food: Most of the food eaten by the Abenaki came from farming. The women of the tribe generally tended the crops, which included corn, gourds, squash, and beans. The men would hunt small animals that lived in the area, including deer, rabbits, and moose.

Clothing: Abenaki men wore breechcloth and leather pants. The woman wore deerskin skirts. In cold weather, they wore ponchos to stay warm. Both men and women would sometimes wear a headband with a feather in it. At times, an Abenaki chief might wear a feather headdress.

Art: The Abenaki are known for their art that includes quillwork, beadwork, and baskets made of bark from the ash tree. Like many other tribes, they made and traded wampum, using white and purple beads made of shells. Wampum was made into bracelets and belts that often had a design that told a story. The children played with dolls made out of cornhusks.

French and Indian War, came to an end in 1763, when the French signed the Treaty of Paris. Under this **treaty**, France surrendered to Great Britain virtually all of the land it had controlled in eastern North America. In the end, the conflict in the New World between the French and the British was a disaster for the Native Americans of New Hampshire. Many were killed in the fighting, and many more fled to Canada. By the end of the eighteenth century, nearly all of them were gone.

During the late 1600s, the population of New Hampshire grew quite slowly and the people were governed for much of the time from Massachusetts. As late as 1732, there were only thirty-eight towns in all, with a total population of about 12,500. In 1741, New Hampshire finally got its own colonial governor, Benning Wentworth, who remained in office for twenty-five years. During

Benning Wentworth served as New Hampshire's first colonial governor.

his tenure, he commissioned the building of Fort Wentworth in Northumberland. The fort played an important role during the Revolutionary War as troops there protected northern New Hampshire from British troops stationed in Canada. In one controversial move, Wentworth began issuing land grants in an area west of the Connecticut River that was also claimed by the Province of New York. This area would later become Vermont. He also donated land that would become Dartmouth College. Under Wentworth and his nephew John Wentworth, who followed him as governor, the colony developed more rapidly, although it remained a rugged frontier region.

Dartmouth College, located in Hanover, is one of the oldest colleges in the United States. It opened its doors in 1769 as a school for young Native Americans. Today it is one of eight colleges that make up the Ivy League. These schools compete against each other in sports and are among the nation's top-ranked colleges academically. The name "Ivy League" was introduced by sportswriters back in the 1920s, in reference to older schools. The other Ivy League colleges are Harvard, Yale, Princeton, Columbia, Brown, and Cornell universities and the University of Pennsylvania. Famous people who went to Dartmouth College include writer Theodor Geisel, best known as Dr. Seuss; poet Robert Frost; and actress Meryl Streep.

By 1775, the people of Britain's thirteen colonies had been unhappy with British rule for a long time. Their anger at having very little say in colonial government and having to pay high taxes—some of which were meant to cover the cost of fighting the French—led to the American Revolution.

The town of Portsmouth, New Hampshire's first capital, played a big role in the American Revolution. The American navy built warships in its shipyards. One of these was the *Ranger*, which war hero Captain John Paul Jones sailed across the Atlantic Ocean to make a daring attack on Britain itself. But many people in Portsmouth were loyalists and sided with the British. That was one of the reasons why the state capital was moved to Concord in 1808.

New Hampshire native John Stark led colonial troops to victory in the Battle of Bennington.

Making a Cornhusk Doll

Corn was an important crop for many Native American tribes. In addition to using the corn for food, many children in the Pennacook and Abenaki tribes made dolls out of cornhusks, the leaves on the outside of the vegetable. Now you can make your own cornhusk doll.

What You Need

Several corn husks—green (not dried) husks are best. You can take these off fresh ears of corn. Or if you only have dry husks available, soak them in water until they are soft.

String

Scissors

Yarn or corn silk, and felt

What to Do

- Lay four or six husks in a stack. Always use an even number of husks.
- Using your string, tie the husks together about an inch from the top.
- Separate the husks, folding them down the way you would peel a banana, so the string is covered.
- Tie more string around the husks about an inch from the new top to form the doll's head.
- Roll a single husk into a tube-like shape, and tie both ends to form the doll's arms.
- Stick the arm husk through the doll's body, below the head.
- Tie string around the middle of the body to create the doll's waist.
- Trim the bottom of the husks to an even length if you want your doll to have a skirt.
- If you want your doll to have pants, separate the husks below the waist into two legs and tie at knees and ankles.
- Decorate your doll with yarn or corn silk for hair and felt for clothes.

The first attack against the British government actually came in New Hampshire, four months before the shots fired by the colonists at Lexington and Concord, Massachusetts, opened the American Revolution. On December 14, 1774, four hundred men took over the lightly defended Fort William and Mary, on the island of New Castle. They overcame the British, without serious casualties on either side,

and captured weapons and one hundred barrels of "the king's gunpowder." Some of that powder was probably used against the British six months later, at the Battle of Bunker Hill, in Massachusetts. New Hampshire militiamen fought in that battle, inflicting heavy casualties. Meanwhile, in January 1776, New Hampshire became the first of the colonies to write its own constitution and form an independent government.

New Hampshire sent three regiments to join the colonists' Continental Army. In all, about five thousand men from New Hampshire fought in the American Revolution. John Stark, a New Hampshire native, was a major figure in the war. He led the American forces to a decisive victory at the Battle of Bennington, fought near that Vermont town in August 1777. Many years later, as an elderly man, Stark was invited to a reunion for veterans of that battle. He was too ill to attend, but he sent a letter with a toast to be given there. It said, "Live free or die; death is not the worst of evils." The first part of this toast became the official state motto in 1945.

The Deciding Vote

When the war ended, New Hampshire still had an important role to play. On June 21, 1788, it became the ninth state to approve the United States Constitution. New Hampshire's vote meant that two-thirds of the states had accepted the Constitution, thus ensuring that it would become the law of the land.

During the next few decades, New Hampshire prospered through farming, logging, shipbuilding, and trade. The population grew, and manufacturing industries began to develop. In fact, many people in New Hampshire, and the rest of New England, opposed the War of 1812, against Great Britain, fearing it would interfere with shipping and trade.

The state government did not always cooperate to aid the war effort. But the New Hampshire state militia joined in the fighting, especially around the St. Lawrence River. In addition, some New Hampshirites became "privateers," whose ships acted as a sort of private navy, attacking enemy ships at sea. These privateers focused largely on intercepting British supply ships and taking the goods they were trying to send to their troops in the colonies.

In 1832, a land dispute led to an interesting **predicament** for residents in a small region in the northern part of New Hampshire. Both Canada and the United States claimed the area, about 200,000 acres (80,937 hectares) near the Canadian border, as their own. Both countries demanded taxes from the residents there. In response, the people who lived there declared themselves an independent nation called the Republic of Indian Stream, complete with their own constitution and congress. In 1835, the New Hampshire militia gained control of the area, and in 1836, the British gave up their claim to the land, turning ownership over to New Hampshire. The region later became known as the town of Pittsburg.

Question of Slavery

Slaves were present in New Hampshire as early as 1645. Because New Hampshire was one of only a few colonies that did not impose a tax on transporting slaves, many traders brought slaves through this area before moving them to other colonies. In the early 1770s, there were about 675 black slaves in New Hampshire. Most of them escaped or were freed by British troops during the Revolution. But the slave trade continued to operate out of Portsmouth until the early 1800s, and the state continued to have small numbers of slaves for some years. Census records show that in the first decades of the nineteenth century, fewer than a dozen slaves lived in the state at any time.

Most New Hampshirites believed slavery was wrong and did not want to see it extended into new territories in the West. In fact, New Hampshire laws at the time were considered quite liberal toward free black people, even giving black men the right to vote. However, many New Hampshire residents were afraid disagreements between Northern and Southern states over slavery would cause the country to break up. One of them was Daniel Webster,

Daniel Webster was born in this building in Franklin.

a statesman well known for his stirring speeches. In his later years as a US senator from Massachusetts, he played a key role in bringing about the so-called Compromise of 1850—a group of five laws that tried to patch over differences between Northerners and Southerners. The compromise allowed a large area of the West to be settled with the question of slavery left open, but also allowed California to enter the Union as a free state. (The Union was another term for the United States used at that time.) To satisfy Southerners, Congress also made it easier to capture slaves who had escaped to the North.

Another politician who tried to get around the slavery controversy was Franklin Pierce, a New Hampshirite who served as president of the United States from 1853 to 1857. He supported the Kansas-Nebraska Act of 1854, which allowed settlers in the Kansas-Nebraska territory to decide for themselves whether to allow slavery in the territory. But it led to fierce conflict between pro-slavery and anti-slavery forces, and tensions between the North and the South only got worse. On April 12, 1861, after Abraham Lincoln had become president, Southern troops fired on Fort Sumter, in South Carolina, beginning the Civil War.

10 KEY CITIES ★ ★ ★

Concord

Dover

1. Manchester: population 109,565

New Hampshire's largest city is also ranked as one of the most affordable and tax-friendly places to live in the United States, making it an attractive place start a business. Manchester was the home to the now-**defunct** Amoskeag textile mills.

2. Nashua: population 86,494

Located between the Merrimack and Nashua Rivers, Nashua is called "Gate City" because it sits between Boston and Concord. In 1838, it was home to New Hampshire's first locomotive engine, owned by the Nashua & Lowell Railroad.

3. Concord: population 42,695

The capital of New Hampshire is also the location of the state's only law school, the University of New Hampshire School of Law. Before Europeans arrived, Concord was populated by many Pennacook. Today, several health care and insurance companies are located there.

4. Derry: population 33,109

Derry was home to a bustling shoe manufacturing industry for much of the early twentieth century. When many of those factories moved, Derry's economy suffered. But in 1963, Interstate Highway 93 opened near Derry and within a decade, the town's population doubled.

5. Dover: population 29,987

Dover is part of New Hampshire's Seacoast region, the southeast portion of the state on the Atlantic Ocean. The town's Woodman Museum features four historic buildings, including an original colonial garrison house.

6. Rochester: population 29,752

Rochester is known as Lilac City because of the flowers that bloom abundantly each year. In the spring, Rochester hosts a Lilac Family Fun Festival. Other attractions include the Rochester Opera House and the Rochester Fair.

7. Salem: population 28,776

Salem is the site of some of New Hampshire's most popular tourist attractions, including America's Stonehenge and Canobie Lake Park. The park was opened in 1902 as a "trolley park," a destination built by a railway company to promote their business.

8. Merrimack: population 25,494

Merrimack is made up of four villages: Merrimack Village, Thornton's Ferry, Reed's Ferry, and South Merrimack. The invention of the automobile turned Merrimack from a quiet agricultural village to a bustling suburb of Boston and nearby New Hampshire cities.

9. Hudson: population 24,467

Hudson is home to Alvirne High School's Wilbur H. Palmer Vocational-Technical Center. This school teaches students real-world skills that can be used in many jobs and features several student-run businesses, including a bank..

10. Londonderry: population 24,129

This town is just south of Manchester and west of Derry in southern New Hampshire. Londonderry has preserved a large amount of land for outdoor recreational use, including Scobie Pond, Musquash Conservation Area, and several athletic fields.

Rochester

America's Stonehenge at Salem

The Granite State contributed many soldiers to the Union forces in the Civil War, including these from the Third New Hampshire Infantry.

Close to forty thousand soldiers from New Hampshire fought in the Civil War. The state supplied eighteen infantry regiments, two cavalry units, two artillery units, and several companies of sharpshooters. They joined in raids on South Carolina and fought in major battles such as the first and second Battles of Manassas (or Bull Run), Antietam, and Gettysburg. Thousands died. One of the earliest Northern soldiers to be killed was a New Hampshirite—Luther C. Ladd, from the town of Alexandria. Ladd had joined the Massachusetts Sixth Regiment as a volunteer. He was among four soldiers to be fatally wounded when mobs attacked the regiment as it marched through Baltimore, just a few days into the war. There were no Civil War battles fought in New Hampshire.

After the Civil War

The Civil War ended in a Union victory in 1865 and resulted in the end of slavery throughout the United States. When New Hampshire's soldiers came home after the war, they returned to a state that was changing fast. Factories and mills were rapidly replacing family farms. By the mid-1870s, more than half the workers in the state held manufacturing jobs, and the state was producing everything from shoes to window glass to pianos. One of New Hampshire's most important industries was textile (cloth) manufacturing. The largest textile mill in the world at that time was the one built by the Amoskeag Manufacturing Company in Manchester. In the early 1900s, Amoskeag employed about seventeen thousand men, women, and children.

Many New Hampshirites had died in the Civil War, and many others moved west in the decades after the war seeking new opportunities. The state's mills and factories needed more workers, and large numbers of immigrants arrived from Europe and Canada. By 1900, two out of every five New Hampshirites were immigrants or the children of immigrants.

The White Mountains region was also beginning to be developed. Railroad companies laid tracks into the mountains, to haul out lumber and paper from the saw mills and pulp mills of towns such as Berlin. The same trains brought in a new resource: tourists. They came to visit the new resort hotels that were being built and to try a winter sport Americans had just discovered: skiing. Some of these visitors liked the state so much that they moved there. The state's population was on the rise.

The Amoskeag Manufacturing Company, once the largest textile manufacturer in the world, shut down in 1936.

The Merrimack River swamped Manchester in the flood of 1936.

Modern Times

In the twentieth century, New Hampshire hosted a peace conference that ended a war on the other side of the world. On September 5, 1905, the Treaty of Portsmouth was signed—not actually at Portsmouth, but at Wentworth by the Sea, an elegant hotel on nearby New Castle Island. The treaty, which ended the Russo-Japanese War—a two-year conflict between Russia and Japan—was negotiated by President Theodore Roosevelt and led to his receiving the Nobel Peace Prize. Some historians believe Roosevelt chose New Hampshire as the site for the peace conference because the weather was cooler there than in Washington, DC. The treaty is still considered one of the most important moments in modern relations between the United States, Russia, and Japan.

When the United States entered World War I, in 1917, New Hampshire industries made important contributions to the war effort. The state produced uniforms, shoes, weapons, and ships—especially submarines, which were then a new invention—for the nation's armed forces. More than twenty thousand New Hampshirites served in World War I.

The years after World War I were difficult for New Hampshire. The textile industry was hit hard by competition from Southern states. Then, in 1929, the stock market crashed and New Hampshire, along with the rest of the nation, was plunged into the Great Depression.

During the Depression, which lasted through the 1930s, New Hampshirites suffered from poverty and unemployment. Their problems were made even worse by natural disasters, including a terrible flood in 1936 and a hurricane in 1938. Winds gusted to 163 miles per hour (262 kmh) and knocked out a part of a trestle on the Cog Railway on Mount Washington. Rain from the New England Hurricane also caused flooding worse than that seen just two years earlier. By the mid-1930s, even the great Amoskeag mill had shut down. The vast buildings used by Amoskeag were eventually renovated and today are home to offices, art studios, branches of local colleges, and the Millyard Museum. The museum commemorates the history of Amoskeag and textile manufacturing in Manchester in general.

First Potato

Londonderry played an important role in the American history of one of our most popular foods, the potato. It is believed that Scots-Irish immigrants living in Londonderry planted the nation's first potato crop there around 1719. From there, the crop spread across the country.

The Allies sent representatives to the Mount Washington Hotel in 1944 to create a world financial system that would start when World War II ended.

World War II, in which the United States fought from 1941 to 1945, helped revive the state's industries. The shipyards of Portsmouth built as many as two submarines a week. More than twenty thousand people found jobs there. Many of the workers were women because thousands of New Hampshire's men were serving in the armed forces during the war. The United States Army Air Forces, the US's military aviation service during World War II, also established many airfields in New Hampshire. These airfields were places where pilots and crew could train on bombers and fighter jets. Though most of these airfields are no longer used for their original purpose, many were converted to municipal airports, and others were used by the United States Air Force as bases during the Cold War.

New Hampshire schoolteacher Christa McAuliffe died in the explosion of the *Challenger*.

In July 1944, as World War II was nearing an end, government officials from all over the world gathered in the White Mountains, at the Mount Washington Hotel in Bretton Woods, to create a new financial system for the postwar world. More than 730 delegates from all forty-four Allied nations attended the conference. The result was the International Monetary Fund and the World Bank. These institutions are still the foundations of the international financial system.

The years after World War II were also a time of change in New Hampshire. The state's economy grew as new types of industry arrived, drawn by skilled workers and low taxes. In the 1950s, small manufacturing companies—often making electronic equipment— began to take the place of textile mills and shoe factories. By the 1970s, "high-tech" companies, such as computer manufacturers, were becoming an important part of the

The Seabrook Nuclear Power plant generated protests in New Hampshire.

state's economy. Sanders Associates, a defense manufacturer, and Digital Equipment Corporation were two major companies that helped lead this technology-based revival in the later part of the twentieth century.

On May 5, 1961, astronaut Alan Shepard, a native of Derry, became the first American in space, piloting the *Freedom 7* spacecraft. Ten years later, he was the fifth American and the oldest person to walk on the moon. During that mission, he hit two golf balls on the surface of the moon. On January 28, 1986, Christa McAuliffe, a Concord high school teacher, became the first private citizen to participate in a spaceflight. Tragically, however, she was killed, along with the six astronauts aboard, when their *Challenger* space shuttle exploded shortly after takeoff. A planetarium in Concord is now named after both of these New Hampshire space pioneers.

In recent years, New Hampshire has played an important role in

Downhill Pioneers

Known for its snowy winters and majestic mountains, New Hampshire is home to the nation's longest continually operating ski club. The Nansen Ski Club was created in 1872 in Berlin as the Berlin Mills Ski Club, and was given its current name in the 1920s after explorer Fridtjof Nansen.

national politics, as it is home to the country's first primary election, the race that helps determine the candidates who will run for president.

Changes have not always been easy for the people of New Hampshire. In the early 1970s, for example, a power company announced that it was planning to build a nuclear reactor at Seabrook, on the Atlantic Coast, to generate electricity. Some people in the state wanted the reactor built to supply electrical energy for homes and businesses. But others feared the new technology, believing the reactor was dangerous and might damage the environment. After a political and legal battle that lasted seventeen years, the Seabrook nuclear reactor began producing electricity in 1990. It was completed ten years later than expected.

Despite such concerns, New Hampshire in the early twenty-first century is generally doing well. Many jobs in manufacturing and other sectors of the economy were lost in the state during the nationwide recession that began in late 2007. But by 2010 new jobs, especially in travel and other service industries, had already made up for half of those losses. With its attractive landscape, low taxes, and relatively low cost of living, New Hampshire appears poised for a bright future.

Wind Power

Mount Washington once held the world record for the fastest wind gust ever recorded: 231 miles per hour [372 kmh] on April 12, 1934. The record fell in 1996 when an unmanned station in Australia recorded 253 miles per hour [407 kmh], but Mount Washington's record still stands as the highest wind gust ever observed by humans.

10 KEY DATES IN STATE HISTORY

1. 1614

John Smith explores the mouth of the Piscataqua River and the Isles of Shoals. He was the first to call this region "New England."

2. 1623

English colonists establish a settlement called Pannaway Plantation, near the present-day town of Rye on Odiorne's Point.

3. November 7, 1629

An earlier land grant to Sir Ferdinando Gorges and Captain John Mason is divided in two. Mason names his portion New Hampshire.

4. December 14, 1774

A raid on the British fort on New Castle Island marks the first outbreak of hostilities between colonists and the British, leading into the American Revolution.

5. June 2, 1784

New Hampshire's state constitution, after years of writing, goes into effect, making it the first colony to create its own independent government.

6. March 4, 1853

Franklin Pierce is sworn in as fourteenth president of the United States. Pierce was born in Hillsborough and attended the Phillips Exeter Academy.

7. December 24, 1935

The Amoskeag Manufacturing Company in Manchester declares bankruptcy after years of declining sales. The mill closes with fewer than one thousand employees.

8. May 3, 2003

The famous Old Man of the Mountain rock formation collapses. The formation could not be rebuilt.

9. June 7, 2003

Gene Robinson is elected Bishop of the New Hampshire diocese. He is the first openly gay Episcopal bishop, and his election stirs controversy worldwide.

10. October 18, 2014

The annual Keene Pumpkin Festival turns violent when thousands of attendees begin rioting. Extensive damage to public and private property and many injuries resulted.

The outdoors and the pace of life
attract people to New Hampshire.

The People

When Europeans began exploring the region that is now New Hampshire, in the 1500s and 1600s, it was home to thousands of Native Americans. Most of New Hampshire's Native Americans lost their lives to disease or were forced off their land by European settlement. Until the mid-1800s, most of the people of European descent who lived in the region were typical New England "Yankees"—mainly people of English or Welsh ancestry. But after that, larger numbers of immigrants began arriving from various European nations.

In 1790, at the time the first US Census was taken, there were more than 140,000 people living in New Hampshire. More than two-thirds were of Welsh or English descent. Nearly all the rest were Irish, Scottish, Dutch, French, or German. There were about 150 slaves.

From the mid-nineteenth to the early twentieth century, immigrants flooded into New Hampshire from Europe, especially to work in the state's fast-growing factories and mills. The largest number of new immigrants at first came from Ireland. But later in the 1800s, many people began to arrive from Germany and the Scandinavian countries of northern Europe. In the early 1900s immigrants came in large numbers from other European countries as well, including Greece, Russia, Poland, Austria, Italy, and Lithuania.

Influx From French Canada

The largest number of new immigrants during this time, however, came not from a European nation but from right next door: the Canadian province of Quebec. These people spoke French and most were Roman Catholic. Although they were drawn to the economic opportunity New Hampshire offered, the first French Canadians who came to New Hampshire remained closely attached to their distinctive culture and way of life. They often chose to live in separate areas, called **Petits Canadas** ("Little Canadas"), with their own French-language schools, churches, and businesses. Today, people of French-Canadian ancestry are much more a part of the daily life of the state. But many of them preserve their own traditions as well, and some still speak French at home.

For many of New Hampshire's immigrant residents in the late nineteenth and early twentieth centuries, social clubs were a way to build community and more fully integrate into their new state and country. Native New Hampshirites took part in fraternal organizations as well, including the Masons and the Grange. Unfortunately, some anti-immigrant feelings among Americans prevented new arrivals from joining these groups, so they formed their own. Many young French Canadian immigrants were part of a group called L'Association Catholique de Jeunesse Franco-Americaine, or the Association of Young French-Canadian Catholics. This group was modeled after similar organizations in Quebec. Although the groups in Quebec were intended for young people, there was such a need for community gatherings in New Hampshire that many people belonged to the group well into adulthood.

The first residents of New Boston, New Hampshire, moved from Boston, Massachusetts. They gave the town its name in 1751.

Polish immigrants joined social clubs as well. Many of these groups were centered around Polish-American churches. The Pulaski Brotherhood and the Kosciuszko Brotherhood were named for notable Polish-Americans who fought in the Revolutionary War. Naming the organizations after these two people was a way for Polish immigrants to feel a connection to both the roots of their home country and their new home in America.

Between 1900 and 1920, about 350,000 Greeks came to the United States. Many came to escape political and economic hardship. Most came from the country's southern peninsula, the northern province of Macedonia, and the islands of the Aegean and Ionian Seas. By 1920, there were three thousand Greeks living in Manchester and about 1,200 in Nashua. Greek workers made up about 10 percent of the workforce at the Amoskeag mills. Other Greek immigrants started their own small businesses or worked for other shops in their new communities. The influence of Greek culture on New Hampshire's architecture can be seen at Concord's Mary Baker Eddy House, which is built in the Greek revival style.

African Americans also lived in the region that is now New Hampshire, as long ago as the mid-1600s. Prior to the Civil War, most were slaves, and their numbers remained small. In the late 1800s, discriminatory attitudes led many of New Hampshire's biggest employers—mills and factories—to hire white immigrants rather than African Americans. Instead, many African Americans were self-employed as barbers or housekeepers. These economic difficulties caused many African-American New Hampshirites to leave the state in search of employment in places like Boston or New York City. Over the past few decades, some African Americans from other states have moved to New Hampshire, adding to the population mix.

The People Today

New Hampshire is still less diverse, ethnically and culturally, than most states. About 94 percent of New Hampshirites are Caucasian, or white. About half the people trace their ancestry to the British Isles alone. Hispanics, who may be of any race, make up less than 3 percent of the total population. African Americans make up slightly more than 1 percent, and Asian Americans make up slightly more than 2 percent. The Native American population is small, numbering a few thousand.

1. Dan Brown

This author, most famous for his bestselling novel *The Da Vinci Code*, was born and raised in Exeter on the campus of Phillips Exeter Academy. Brown's father was a math teacher at the school.

Dan Brown

2. Mary Baker Eddy

Eddy, the founder of the Christian Science movement, was born in Bow in 1821. Christian Scientists believe that illness and injury should be treated with prayer alone. Eddy founded *The Christian Science Monitor.*

3. Robert Frost

Robert Frost was born in 1874 in San Francisco but lived most of his life in New Hampshire. The Robert Frost Farm near Derry, where he lived until his death in 1963, is a popular tourist destination.

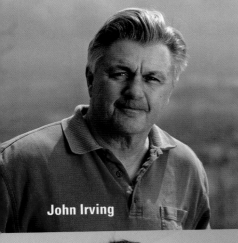

John Irving

4. John Irving

Born and educated in Exeter, John Irving has written thirteen novels, including *A Prayer for Owen Meany* and *The World According to Garp*. He won an Oscar for his screenplay of *The Cider House Rules*. A wrestler and a coach, he was inducted into the National Wrestling Hall of Fame in 1992.

5. Seth Meyers

The host of *Late Night with Seth Meyers* was born in 1973 and raised in Bedford. Meyers joined the cast of *Saturday Night Live* in 2001 and was head writer from 2006 until 2014, when he left to host *Late Night.*

Seth Meyers

NEW HAMPSHIRE

6. Bode Miller

Born in 1977 in Easton, Bode Miller grew up near Cannon Mountain and began skiing at the age of three. He is one of the best American alpine skiers ever. By 2014, he had gained six Olympic medals and thirty-three World Cup victories.

7. Mandy Moore

This singer, actress, and fashion designer was born in Nashua in 1984. She is known for songs such as "Candy" and "So Real," and for her movie roles in *A Walk to Remember* and *The Princess Diaries*.

8. Alan Shepard

Alan Shepard was a rear admiral in the US Navy and the first American launched into space. He reached an altitude of 116 miles (187 km). He walked on the moon as a member of the *Apollo 14* crew and won the Congressional Medal of Honor.

9. David Souter

Souter was born in Massachusetts in 1939 but moved to Weare when he was eleven and went on to attend Concord High School. He was appointed to the Supreme Court by President George H. W. Bush in 1990 and served until 2009.

10. Earl Tupper

The containers used by millions to store lunch and leftovers—Tupperware—was the creation of a businessman from Berlin. Earl Tupper developed the lightweight plastic while working for the DuPont Chemical Company and launched the Tupperware Plastics Company in 1938.

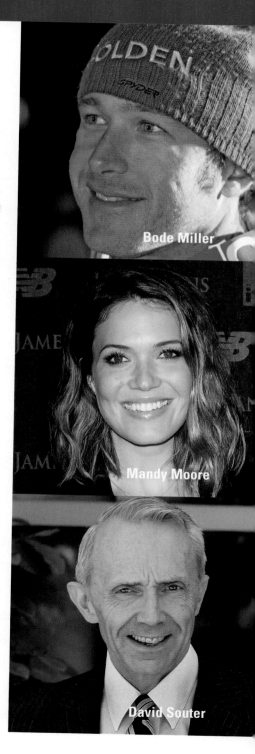

Bode Miller

Mandy Moore

David Souter

Who Are the New Hampshirites

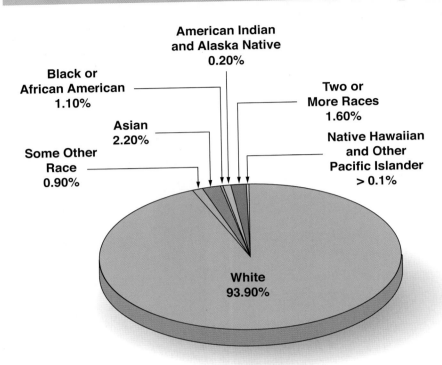

American Indian and Alaska Native
0.20%

Black or African American
1.10%

Asian
2.20%

Some Other Race
0.90%

Two or More Races
1.60%

Native Hawaiian and Other Pacific Islander
> 0.1%

White
93.90%

Total Population
1,316,470

Hispanic or Latino (of any race):
• 36,704 people (2.8%)

Note: The pie chart shows the racial breakdown of the state's population based on the categories used by the U.S. Bureau of the Census. The Census Bureau reports information for Hispanics or Latinos separately, since they may be of any race. Percentages in the pie chart may not add to 100 because of rounding.

Source: US Bureau of the Census, 2010 Census

On the other hand, one-fourth of the people in New Hampshire are of French or French-Canadian descent, a much larger proportion than in most states. In addition, like other states, New Hampshire in the past few decades has been welcoming increased numbers of immigrants from countries outside of Europe. Close to a quarter of all foreign-born residents in New Hampshire today come from Latin America, and more than a quarter are from Asia. While immigrants continue to arrive in significant numbers from Canada, Germany, and Greece, others hail from India, China, Vietnam, and the Philippines, as well as from the Dominican Republic, Mexico, and Brazil.

People from other states and countries all contribute to New Hampshire's cultural diversity. Some new residents had visited or attended school in New Hampshire and later decided to move there. Many move to the state to enjoy its peaceful surroundings.

Claudio Marcus, who came to the United States from the South American nation of Chile when he was twelve, is one of those people. About ten years ago, he and his wife left their home in Baltimore, Maryland, to settle in the small New Hampshire village of Andover. "We came here looking for the things everybody wants," he says. "Good schools, safe neighborhoods, a great place for our kids to grow up. And we definitely found those things here." If he had any doubts about being welcomed in a state with few Spanish-speaking residents, they went away quickly. "We'd only been here a few weeks when one of our new neighbors invited us to our first town meeting."

Keeping Tradition Alive

New Hampshire is known for its neighborly spirit and small, close-knit population centers. There are no cities as big as New York, Boston, or Providence. The state's three largest cities—Manchester, Nashua, and Concord—have a combined population of less than 250,000 people. And most New Hampshirites live in smaller towns and villages. Many residents make their homes in communities where their families have lived for generations.

Some fear that this small-town spirit is losing ground. A good number of New Hampshirites now commute from Portsmouth and the other towns along the coast to jobs in the Boston area, which is only about an hour's drive to the south. Others "telecommute"—using technologies such as webcams and the Internet to work from their homes. The result, some longtime New Hampshirites complain, is that the Seacoast Region is becoming just another suburb of Boston.

But the seacoast—and the rest of New Hampshire—has not changed all that much. While the state has its share of shopping malls and fast-food restaurants, the landscape remains, for the most part, quiet, peaceful, and unspoiled. There is a good reason: That is the way many longtime residents and visitors alike want New Hampshire to stay.

There are many traditional New England houses and shops in North Conway.

Fun and Culture

The people of New Hampshire are very interested in preserving the state's traditions. This is evident at the many summer festivals and fall fairs that celebrate New Hampshire's old small-town ways, as well as in the historic monuments, museums, and celebrations that attract visitors to the state. It is evident, too, in New Hampshire's centuries-old love of the arts.

Festivals, events, and fairs are also a way for New Hampshire residents to celebrate American history and the culture and heritage of the immigrants who settled there years ago. In July, the town of Berlin celebrates its past with French-Canadian crafts and a re-creation of a nineteenth-century logging camp. One of the highlights is a traditional "bean hole supper," where the beans are cooked in a big hole in the ground. Every September, the New Hampshire Highland Games in Lincoln celebrates all things Scottish—from kilts and tartans to bagpipes and fiddles. It is said to be the largest such event in the Northeast. The American Independence Festival in the seacoast town of Exeter celebrates the American Revolution in July with eighteenth-century costumes and music, as well as a battle reenactment.

Fall festivals and Halloween parades are popular in New Hampshire.

The Deerfield Fair is the oldest event of its kind in New England. This agricultural fair, held in late September and early October, has been featuring livestock shows, sheepdog trials, and many other traditional rural events since 1876. Children's festivals are another favorite pastime. The Annual Hampton Beach Children's Festival, held in August, includes such features as a magic show, a sandcastle competition, and free ice cream. The climax is a giant costume parade for kids. The Somersworth International Children's Festival, held in the southeastern New Hampshire city of Somersworth each June, attracts kids of all ages with music, fireworks, crafts, animals, and games.

For four days in July, the skies above the town of Hillsborough are filled with brightly colored hot air balloons for the Hillsborough Balloon Festival and Fair. Visitors and locals alike can take in this amazing sight and also enjoy carnival rides, firefighters' contests, and a mud bog pull. For almost eighty years, the craftspeople of New Hampshire have been showing off their best work—jewelry, pottery, woodworking, and more—at the League of New Hampshire Craftsmen's Fair, now held every August at Sunapee State Park in Newbury. The first Craftsmen's Fair was held in 1933.

New Hampshire Motor Speedway hosts drivers at the top two levels of stock car racing for two weekends each year. The NASCAR events are held in July and September, and they attract nearly one hundred thousand fans each day to the facility in Loudon.

New Hampshire has welcomed writers, painters, and other artists for many years. Among the creative people who have lived in the Granite State are the poet Robert Frost, the novelists J. D. Salinger and John Irving, and the sculptors Daniel Chester French and Augustus Saint-Gaudens. The writer Sarah Josepha Hale, a Newport native, wrote the famous children's rhyme "Mary Had a Little Lamb." The state is also the home of the MacDowell Colony, an artists' retreat near Peterborough founded in 1907 by the composer Edward MacDowell. It offers writers, painters, and composers from all over the country a quiet place to create art. While staying at the MacDowell Colony, Thornton Wilder wrote his famous play *Our Town*, which depicts small-town New Hampshire life in the early 1900s.

What do most New Hampshirites have in common? The people—both longtime residents and newcomers—seem to like the New Hampshire way of life. After all, that is why many of them came to New Hampshire in the first place.

10 KEY EVENTS ★

Candlelight Stroll

Deerfield Fair

1. Candlelight Stroll

The Strawbery Banke area of Portsmouth is home to this December event that features historic homes lit with hundreds of candles. Through featured exhibits and live re-enactments, attendees can get a glimpse at the history of New Hampshire's oldest waterfront neighborhood.

2. Deerfield Fair

The oldest event of its kind in New England, this agricultural fair, held in late September or early October, has been featuring livestock shows, sheepdog trials, and many other traditional rural events since 1876.

3. Fields of Lupine Festival

Each June, several towns in New Hampshire celebrate the lupine blossom with a three-week festival. Events include historic tours, garden workshops, contests, concerts, and a pageant. Artists and crafters display their work.

4. Great North Woods Sled Dog Challenge

This three-day race takes participants from Milan, north to Pittsburg—almost the Canadian border—and back down to Colebrook. The end of the races features a celebratory winter carnival.

5. Hampton Beach Seafood Festival

This September festival is considered New England's largest seaside event, featuring more than sixty restaurants from the Seacoast Region. In addition to food, the festival also features arts and crafts vendors, sidewalk sales, and two stages of live entertainment.

6. Hillsboro Balloon Festival and Fair

Hot-air balloons fill the sky above Hillsboro for four days in July. Visitors can enjoy the brightly colored balloons as well as carnival rides, lumberjack and car shows, a road race, and live music.

7. Monadnock International Film Festival

Keene residents honor their love of film and art at this April event that brings together filmmakers, artists, producers, and supporters of the movies. A variety of short and full-length independent films are screened.

8. PaddlePower

PaddlePower is a two-day river adventure in August that gives participants the chance to journey in canoes or kayaks along twenty-five miles of the Connecticut River. The event raises funds for West Central Behavioral Health, which provides mental health services in Grafton and Sullivan Counties.

9. Prescott Parks Arts Festival

Music, art, theater, and dance are celebrated at this July event in Portsmouth near the Piscataqua River. Exhibits include painting, collage, sculpture and photography—all created by New Hampshirites. Awards are given for the best work.

10. RiverFire

Berlin residents celebrate fall and their local heritage at RiverFire, an October festival that features family-friendly events like hay rides and duck races. The event ends with spectacular fire displays on the piers of the Androscoggin River.

Hillsboro Balloon Festival and Fair

Monadnock International Film Festival

Barack Obama visits New Hampshire during one of his successful campaigns for president.

How the Government Works

People in New Hampshire, like Americans in other states, have a voice in how their local, state, and national governments are run. In some ways, New Hampshirites actually have a louder voice. For example, they play a special role in helping to select the president of the United States, because of the New Hampshire primary. They also have a very large number of members in the State House of Representatives—meaning that each member represents a small number of people.

The New Hampshire Primary

Every four years—when it is a presidential election year—in the middle of the cold New Hampshire winter, the nation's attention is focused on this small state. Why? Presidential candidates who win their party's New Hampshire primary election get a good head start in the race for the White House.

The two main political parties—Democrat and Republican—do not officially choose their candidates for president until their national conventions in the summer. But most of the people, or delegates, who vote at these conventions were chosen in state primaries because they agreed to vote for a certain candidate. Many other states have primaries, but New Hampshire's is the first. That makes it especially important, because the candidates who get the most votes gain publicity as "winners," which often helps them in later primaries.

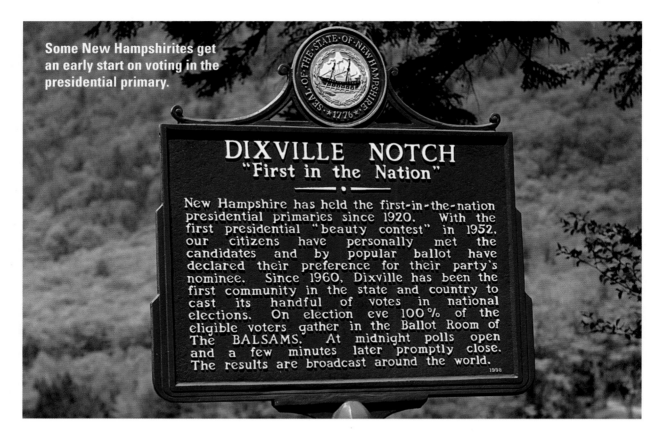

Some New Hampshirites get an early start on voting in the presidential primary.

DIXVILLE NOTCH
"First in the Nation"

New Hampshire has held the first-in-the-nation presidential primaries since 1920. With the first presidential "beauty contest" in 1952, our citizens have personally met the candidates and by popular ballot have declared their preference for their party's nominee. Since 1960, Dixville has been the first community in the state and country to cast its handful of votes in national elections. On election eve 100% of the eligible voters gather in the Ballot Room of The BALSAMS. At midnight polls open and a few minutes later promptly close. The results are broadcast around the world.

1998

Federal and State Government

At the federal, or national, level, New Hampshire, like every state big or small, elects two senators to serve six-year terms in Washington, DC. New Hampshirites also elect two members of the US House of Representatives—one from each of the state's two congressional districts—to serve two-year terms.

The state government is responsible for matters that affect New Hampshire as a whole.

Branches of Government

Executive

The New Hampshire governor supervises state government, plans the budget, and approves or rejects bills that might become law. Unlike in other states, he or she shares important powers with an executive council. Both the governor and the five-member council have a say in spending the state's money, and the council can approve or reject people appointed by the governor, including judges. The governor and executive council are elected to terms of only two years. They do not have term limits—that is, they can be reelected an unlimited number of times.

Legislative

New Hampshire's legislature is called the General Court. It has two parts, or bodies: the Senate, with twenty-four members, and the House of Representatives, with four hundred members. The New Hampshire House of Representatives is the largest state legislative body in the country, and one of the largest legislative bodies in the world. Members of the General Court pass the laws that govern New Hampshire. They are elected for two-year terms, with no term limits.

Judicial

New Hampshire's judges are appointed by the governor and may serve until the age of seventy. The state Supreme Court—New Hampshire's highest court—has one chief justice and four associate justices. It hears appeals of decisions made by lower courts, and it can decide whether a state law is allowed under the state constitution. Next come the superior courts. They hold trials for serious crimes and for many civil cases, in which one person, group, or company sues another in a dispute. District courts deal with less serious crimes and with civil disputes involving smaller amounts of money. There is also a family division that handles matters such as divorce and child custody, and a probate court that deals with wills.

How a Bill Becomes a Law

Any member of the state Senate or House can suggest a new law. People who are not members must get a member to sponsor their idea. Each proposed law, or bill, must be written up in the proper form. Once it gets to the Senate or House, the bill is read out loud twice and sent to a committee of lawmakers. Unless there is a two-thirds vote to suspend the rules, the committee must hold a public hearing so that citizens can discuss the measure and suggest changes. The committee then meets and decides, by majority vote, whether to suggest passing the bill as is, passing it with changes (or amendments), sending it for further study, or killing it.

The full House or Senate then debates whatever measures get through the committee. Once a majority of members vote for some version of the bill, it goes to the other body of the legislature to be considered. Both must agree on the exact same bill. If there are differences in the versions of a bill passed by the two bodies, a conference committee tries to find a compromise to present to both bodies for a final vote. If both bodies pass an agreed-upon measure, it goes to the governor.

Bills are debated and passed at the New Hampshire State House.

The governor may accept and sign the bill, in which case it becomes law, or the governor may reject—or veto—it. When the legislature is in session, any bill that is not signed or vetoed in five days automatically becomes law. If a bill is vetoed, it can still become law. To override the veto, two-thirds of the members of each body of the legislature must vote for the bill. When the General Court is not in session, the governor still has five days to sign the bill. But now, if the governor fails to sign it in that time, the bill automatically dies. This is called a pocket veto.

Local Government

New Hampshire's ten counties have some important functions, such as running prisons and hospitals and maintaining courts. But the heart and soul of local politics is the town, and the centuries-old tradition of the town meeting. This is one of the purest forms of "direct democracy" in the world. Direct democracy means that the people themselves—not just their elected representatives—vote on important issues.

The state has 221 communities known as towns, and most of them hold an annual town meeting, usually in March. People can come to the meeting and speak out on issues. The rest of the year, each town is run by a small group of elected representatives, usually known as selectmen (though they can be either men or women).

The state also has thirteen cities. In most of them, major decisions are made by an elected city council. The council chooses one of its members as mayor and hires a city manager to run day-to-day affairs. Other cities, such as Nashua and Manchester, elect a mayor to run their government, along with a board of aldermen.

Taxes

One of the biggest political issues in New Hampshire is taxation. Most states have a state income tax, a state sales tax, or both. The money from these taxes pays for a large part of the state government's expenses.

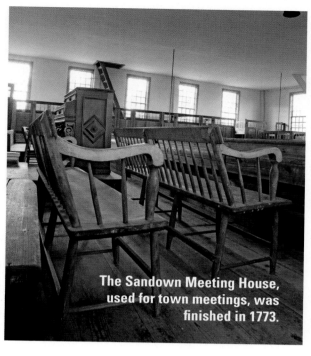

The Sandown Meeting House, used for town meetings, was finished in 1773.

New Hampshire does not have an overall sales tax or an income tax on people's salaries. However, it does have taxes on businesses, on money people make from interest and investments, and on cigarettes, alcohol, and motor fuel. In addition, the state, as well as individual cities and towns, now has a property tax on people's houses and land.

Until the late 1990s, schools were paid for only by local property taxes. As a result, schools in the wealthier towns and cities had more money and were better able to hire good teachers, purchase up-to-date technology and other equipment, and offer after-school athletic and other programs. But the New Hampshire Supreme Court ruled that the state must make sure all students have access to an equally good education. How would the state pay for this? Lawmakers voted to create a state property tax and increase certain other taxes that already existed.

New Hampshire was forty-fourth nationally in the share of state and local taxes its residents paid in 2011. This ranking by the Tax Foundation is based on what part of person's income goes to state and local taxes. The fiftieth, or the least taxed state, was Wyoming.

Revolutionary Law

New Hampshire's motto is "Live Free or Die," and the spirit of that motto is evident in Article 10 of the state's constitution. The article protects the right to revolt against the government and establish a new government if public liberty becomes "manifestly endangered."

Franklin Pierce, US President, 1853–1857

Tensions over the abolitionist movement made Pierce a controversial president, but his previous political career in New Hampshire was considered successful. He served in the US House of Representatives and Senate, and was later appointed US Attorney for the state in 1845. He also ran a well-regarded law practice.

Daniel Webster, Secretary of State, 1841–1843, 1850–1852

This Salisbury native had a political career that spanned about four decades, during which he served as a congressman, senator, and Secretary of State under three presidents. He was known for his powerful speeches and passionate views, though some criticized him for not caring about common people.

Jeanne Shaheen: US Senator, 2009–

Jeanne Shaheen was born in Missouri in 1947 but moved to New Hampshire in the 1970s. In 1996 she became the first woman to be elected governor of the state. In 2008, she became the state's first female US senator and was reelected in 2014. She's the first woman to serve as a governor and in the US Senate.

NEW HAMPSHIRE
YOU CAN MAKE A DIFFERENCE

Contacting Lawmakers

The more you learn about the history of your state and nation and the issues that people face, the more you can become an informed citizen. New Hampshire's tradition of direct participation in politics makes it easier to learn and get involved.

If there is an issue you care about, contact your elected officials by finding their information here: **www.gencourt. state.nh.us/ie/whosmyleg.**

John Lynch vetoed the voting law as governor in 2012.

Voter Law Blocked

In 2014, a controversial law in New Hampshire was changed because of residents speaking their minds on the issue. The law, originally passed in 2012, added text to the state's voter registration form that some considered confusing or unfair. After the law passed, the registration form required voters to agree that they had to adhere to state residency laws. The law defined residents as someone who intended to live in the state for a very long time. Voters were concerned this would discourage people from voting who may have had to move in the near future—for example, students or those in the military. Because the law may have required voters to prove their residency status with a New Hampshire drivers' license, which requires a fee to obtain, some considered it an illegal poll tax that would impede voting for those who could not afford it. The law passed in June 2012, with the New Hampshire legislature overriding then-Governor John Lynch's veto. For two years, residents and voters rights organizations demonstrated their unhappiness with the law. The New Hampshire Civil Liberties Union filed a lawsuit on behalf of four college students and the New Hampshire League of Women Voters. On July 25, 2014, the state Supreme Court decided that the language on the form was confusing and unfair and blocked the law from being enforced.

Many kinds of apples are grown in the orchards of New Hampshire.

Making a Living

The people of New Hampshire have always worked hard. But the ways in which they make their living have changed a great deal in recent years. Agriculture and textile manufacturing have declined in importance, while high-tech manufacturing has grown. Tourism, health care, retail trade, and other so-called service industries are a mainstay of the economy and provide many jobs.

Using Natural Resources

New Hampshire is still known as the Granite State, but granite quarrying no longer employs very many people. Concrete, steel, and other modern building materials have replaced granite in most construction products. Sand and gravel, for building roads, are actually the most important materials mined in the state today.

Farming, the backbone of the New Hampshire economy until the mid-1800s, also has a smaller role today. The state has around four thousand farms, but they account for less than 1 percent of its economic activity. New Hampshire farms produce greenhouse and dairy products and grow crops such as hay, sweet corn, and potatoes. Farmers across the state grow fruits such as apples, blueberries, and strawberries. Maple syrup is also important. Livestock, especially cattle and calves, are a major farm product.

New Hampshire still makes the most of its short coastline, just as it has since the days of Pannaway Plantation. The state's small but valuable fishing industry hauls in cod, flounder, haddock, lobster, and shrimp. The seacoast town of Portsmouth is an important international seaport, handling hundreds of thousands of tons of shipping every year.

The timber industry is heavily concentrated in the northern part of the state. Jobs have declined in recent years, but thousands of New Hampshirites still work for lumber companies. They cut down trees, haul them to mills, and turn them into paper and other products.

Manufacturing

The New Hampshire economy still depends heavily on manufacturing, but as in other states, many manufacturing jobs have been lost in recent years. The manufacturing industry today employs about ninety thousand people, or around 13 percent of the work force. It accounts for about 15 percent of the state's economic output. Traditional New Hampshire specialties, such as clothing and leather goods, long ago declined in importance. The Amoskeag Manufacturing Company in Manchester, once the largest textile manufacturer in the world, fell into decline and ceased operations in 1936. The mill buildings were abandoned for years. Now they have been renovated and contain museums, art galleries, restaurants, and software companies.

Among the state's chief products today are machinery and metal products. But, more and more, New Hampshire's manufacturing industry is built on technology. The technology sector is regarded as a key to growth in the years ahead. The high-tech trend began in the 1970s, when computer manufacturers started moving into the state, attracted by its skilled workers, good working and living conditions, natural beauty, and low taxes. By 2000, New Hampshire was truly a high-tech state, with more than 8 percent of its workers employed in technology-related jobs. Today, southern New Hampshire is an important part of the high-tech corridor that extends from the Boston area. New Hampshire companies make computer components, telecommunications equipment, software, scientific instruments, medical devices, and other highly advanced products.

Many New Hampshirites work at Segway, which is located in Bedford.

Many people today stress the importance of encouraging students to seek careers in science and technology. In 1992, for example, inventor Dean Kamen of Manchester created the FIRST Robotics Competition. FIRST teams—which include high school and college students and industry experts—design and build advanced robots to be pitted against one another. From its beginning in a Manchester school gym, the competition has grown to include some 1,800 teams around the world.

One of the most interesting of the state's high-tech products is the Segway Human Transporter, a two-wheeled, self-balancing, electric-powered "people mover" developed in 2001. Segway Inc. is located in Bedford. On August 28, 2003, a Segway climbed Mount Washington. It took two and a half hours, three riders, and six sets of batteries, but the Segway finally made it up all 7.6 miles (12.2 km) of very steep, not-always-paved roads.

New Hampshire's "tech-friendly" environment is also drawing some of the best scientific minds in the country. In 2003, Dr. Charles Brenner, a leading cancer researcher, moved his entire genetics laboratory from Philadelphia to the little town of Lebanon. "New Hampshire offers me all the facilities I need for my work," he said at the time, "and the quality of life here makes it possible to attract first-class research staff."

★ 10 KEY INDUSTRIES ★

Apples

Biotechnology

1. Apples

New Hampshire farms grow many different kinds of apples, including commonly known varieties like Cortland and Gala. The state's farmers have also cultivated a great number of less common—and still delicious—kinds of apples with names like Granite Beauty and LaFayette's Favorite.

2. Banking and Insurance

Many New Hampshire residents work in insurance and finance. Manchester is the business and financial center of northern New England. Some of the state's largest employers in these industries have operations or headquarters there.

3. Biotechnology

Biotechnology is the use of life-based science to create useful things, like new ways of treating diseases. A 2007 tax credit that aimed to increase high-tech jobs in New Hampshire has helped many biotechnology companies grow and succeed.

4. Dairy Farming

New Hampshire's large areas of open space and farmland make it an ideal location for dairy farming, especially in the Connecticut River Valley and Merrimack River Valley. There are approximately 130 dairy farms in New Hampshire with an average of 115 milking animals per farm.

5. Fishing

Even though New Hampshire has the shortest coastline of all states that border the ocean, a small but steady fishing industry has existed there since the state was founded. Cod, lobster, and shrimp are some of the main products.

NEW HAMPSHIRE

6. Lumber

The lumber industry started in New Hampshire as early as 1634, when tall pines were shipped to England to be used as ship masts. Today, New Hampshire forests produce more than fifty kinds of wood products, from crates to coat hangers.

7. Manufacturing

Traditional manufacturing still plays a key role in the state's economy. Exports of New Hampshire products totaled nearly $4.3 billion in 2013. Plastics, iron, and steel are three key products manufactured in New Hampshire.

8. Mining

Mining is not as large as it was when New Hampshire was nicknamed the Granite State, but there are still about 130 mining operations. Sand, gravel, and concrete are three main resources mined in New Hampshire.

9. Smart Manufacturing/High Technology

The state's legacy of manufacturing continues today with **advanced manufacturing** facilities that produce items such as computer parts and medical devices. This sector, made up of about 2,100 manufacturers and 1,600 high-tech companies, brings in more revenue to New Hampshire than any other industry.

10. Tourism

New Hampshire's beauty makes it a draw year-round for tourists looking to enjoy the outdoors. The Seacoast Region attracts beachgoers, while skiers, snowboarders, and hikers visit the state's mountain ranges.

Lumber

Tourism

Recipe for Garlic Lemon Shrimp

The tourists that flock to New Hampshire's Seacoast Region enjoy fresh seafood caught off the state's shores, including plenty of shrimp. Make your own shrimp with this easy recipe. Have an adult help you with the prep, cutting, and cooking.

What You Need

2 pounds (.9 kg) raw, deveined shrimp

2 tablespoons (29.5 mL) salt

2 teaspoons (9.9 mL) sugar

¼ cup (59 mL) olive oil

¼ cup (59 mL) chopped parsley

1 tablespoon (14.8 mL) grated lemon peel

2 cloves garlic, chopped into tiny pieces

Fresh lemon

What to Do

- Mix the salt and sugar in a bowl. Add the shrimp and toss so it is coated in the mixture. Cover and put in the refrigerator for one hour.

- Remove shrimp and rinse well. Rinse and dry bowl and return shrimp to bowl.

- Add the remaining ingredients and mix to coat.

- Heat a pan on medium heat. Add shrimp to pan.

- Cook for about three to four minutes on each side, until shrimp is completely pink and **opaque** (not see through) in the thickest part.

- Place on a serving plate and squeeze a small amount of fresh lemon over the shrimp.

- Enjoy!

Products and Resources

Trees

Almost 5 million acres (2 million ha)—or more than 80 percent of New Hampshire's land area—is covered by trees. No other state, except Maine, is so heavily wooded. The state's hardwood trees, such as ash, birch, and oak, are used for lumber for construction. Softwoods, such as pine and spruce, are sent to paper mills. The beautiful New Hampshire woods produce many of the nation's Christmas trees.

Biotechnology

One of New Hampshire's fastest-growing industries is biotechnology—or technology that uses living organisms to make or modify certain products or processes. Many New Hampshire companies, most of them located along the seacoast, are doing advanced biotechnology research, which is especially important in developing new medicines.

Computer Software

So many software companies are located in the state that New Hampshire has been called "the silicon state." (Silicon is an element used in computer parts.) Computer-aided design, Internet security, and desktop publishing are just a few of the Granite State's software specialties.

Potatoes

New Hampshire is not as well known for growing potatoes as neighboring Maine. But the first potato in the United States was planted in Londonderry, New Hampshire, in 1719, and potatoes are still a major crop. There are many potato farms in the state, especially in the western part of the White Mountains region.

Maple Syrup

New Hampshire's maple syrup season is short—just a few weeks in March and April—but very sweet. Every year, the state's maple trees produce about 90,000 gallons (340,000 liters) of syrup. That is pretty amazing, when you consider that it takes about forty gallons of tree sap to make just one gallon of syrup.

The Cornish-Windsor Bridge was built in 1866.

Winter Sports

Along with its mountains, forests, lakes, and streams, ice and snow are among New Hampshire's greatest resources. Each winter, residents and visitors alike enjoy skiing, snowboarding, snowshoeing, snow tubing, and snowmobiling, as well as ice skating, ice fishing, and many other outdoor activities. In the process they bring revenue to the New Hampshire economy.

Service Industries

Despite the importance of high-tech and other manufacturing industries, most New Hampshirites actually make their living in service jobs. Doctors, nurses, lawyers, sales-clerks, restaurant workers, and real estate agents perform services for other people. One of the state's biggest service industries is travel and tourism.

New Hampshire ranks among the top ten states in the importance of tourism to the economy. Each year, visitors bring billions of dollars into the state and create tens of thousands of jobs. Among New Hampshire's most famous tourist attractions are its beautiful old covered bridges. More than fifty covered bridges can be found in the state.

This includes one of the longest in the country, the 460-foot (140 m) Cornish-Windsor Bridge, built in 1866.

It is easy to understand why so many people come to New Hampshire for their vacations. The state offers so many pleasures, from the beaches of the seacoast in the summertime to the ski slopes of the White Mountains in the winter. In fact, New Hampshire was the home of the first summer resort in America, in Wolfeboro.

In 1767, John Wentworth, the colonial governor, built a summer home on the shores of the lake that now bears his name. Many other wealthy people did the same, and the first summer resort in America was born.

In the years since then, many people have followed in Governor Wentworth's footsteps and have made New Hampshire one of the most popular tourist destinations in the United States. Every year, hundreds of thousands of people visit the beaches of the seacoast, the lakes and rivers of the Upland, and the mountains and notches of the White Mountains. They come to visit the state's many summer festivals, admire the glorious autumn leaves, and enjoy the winter activities and sports. New Hampshire has many attractions for kids as well as adults. The Children's Museum of New Hampshire, in Dover, offers hands-on exhibits ranging from a dinosaur dig to a yellow submarine. Charmingfare Farm, in Candia, has wolves, reindeer, otters, and other wild animals, along with traditional farm animals and hayrides.

New Hampshirites offer tourists a warm welcome. In fact, you could say that its people are the state's most valuable resource. With their love of tradition, their Yankee ingenuity, their hard work, and their friendly ways, they make sure that New Hampshire remains one of the best places in the country to visit—or to live in.

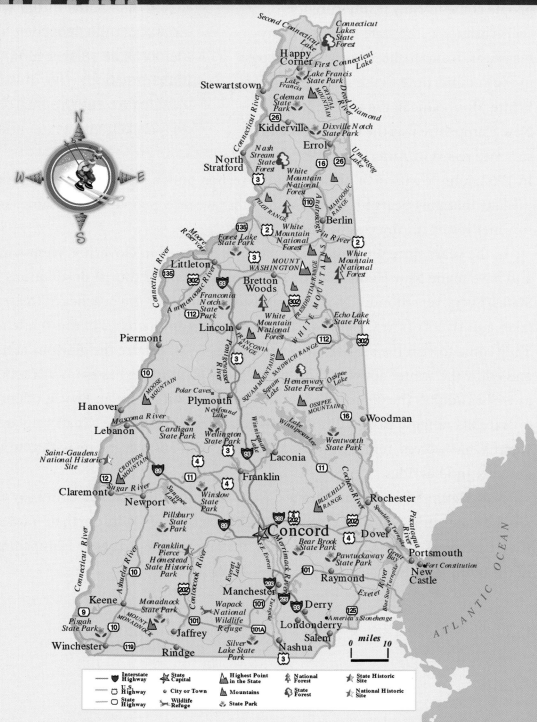

Second Connecticut Lake

Connecticut Lakes State Forest

Happy Corner

First Connecticut Lake

Lake Francis State Park

Stewartstown

Lake Francis

Coleman State Park

Dead Diamond River

CRYSTAL MOUNTAIN

(26) Kidderville

Dixville Notch State Park

Errol

Umbagog Lake

North Stratford

Nash Stream State Forest

(16) (26)

(3)

White Mountain National Forest

PILOT RANGE

(2) White Mountain National Forest

(110) Berlin

MAHOOSUC RANGE

(2)

(135)

Forest Lake State Park

(3)

MOUNT WASHINGTON

White Mountain National Forest

Moore Reservoir

Littleton

(135)

(93) (302)

Bretton Woods

PRESIDENTIAL RANGE

(302)

Echo Lake State Park

WHITE MOUNTAINS

Connecticut River

Ammonoosuc River

Franconia Notch State Park

(112)

White Mountain National Forest

(302)

Lincoln

FRANCONIA RANGE

(112)

Piermont

Pemigewasset River

(3)

SANDWICH RANGE

(10)

MOOSE MOUNTAIN

Polar Caves

Plymouth

SQUAM MOUNTAINS

Squam Lake

Hemenway State Forest

Ossipee Lake

Hanover

Mascoma River

Newfound Lake

OSSIPEE MOUNTAINS

Lebanon

Cardigan State Park

Wellington State Park

Winnisquam Lake

Lake Winnipesaukee

(16) Woodman

Wentworth State Park

Saint-Gaudens National Historic Site

CROYDON MOUNTAIN

(4)

(3)

(93)

Laconia

(11)

Cocheco River

(12)

(89)

(11)

(4)

Franklin

BLUE HILLS RANGE

Rochester

Claremont

Sugar River

Winslow State Park

(4)

Spaulding Turnpike

Dover

Newport

Sunapee Lake

(4)

Piscataqua River

Portsmouth

Pillsbury State Park

(89)

(383) (202) Concord

Bear Brook State Park

(202)

(4)

Fort Constitution

New Castle

Franklin Pierce Homestead State Historic Park

Everett Lake

F.E. Everett

Merrimack River

Pawtuckaway State Park

(01)

Raymond

Great Bay

Exeter River

Keene

Contoocook River

(202)

Wapack National Wildlife Refuge

Manchester

(293)

(101)

(293)

Derry

(93)

America's Stonehenge

(125)

Blue Star Turnpike

(9)

MOUNT MONADNOCK

Monadnock State Park

(101)

(101A)

Londonderry

Salem

Pisgah State Park

(10)

Jaffrey

Silver Lake State Park

(3) Nashua

miles

0   10

Winchester

(119)

Rindge

ATLANTIC OCEAN

Interstate Highway	State Capital	Highest Point in the State	National Forest	State Historic Site
U.S. Highway	City or Town	Mountains	State Forest	National Historic Site
State Highway	Wildlife Refuge	State Park		

NEW HAMPSHIRE

MAP SKILLS

1. What is the name of the river located next to New Hampshire's state capital?

2. What city is located where State Highway 10 meets State Highway 101?

3. Which state forest is located at the most northern point of the state?

4. If you started in North Stratford, and traveled north along the Connecticut River, which city would you reach first?

5. What is the largest body of water located within New Hampshire's borders?

6. What mountain range is located west of Rochester?

7. If you wanted to travel from Plymouth to Mount Washington, in which direction should you travel?

8. How many state parks are shown on the map?

9. Which state highway can take you to both Laconia and Franklin?

10. Which river runs into the Atlantic Ocean?

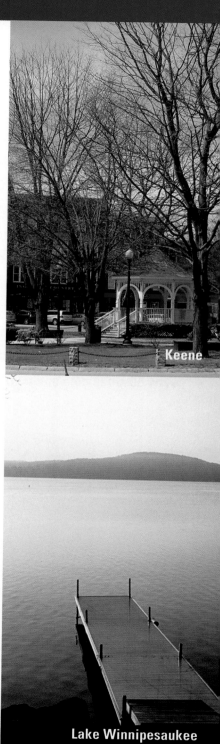

Keene

Lake Winnipesaukee

10. Piscataqua River
9. Route 11
8. Sixteen
7. Northeast
6. Blue Hills Range
5. Lake Winnipesaukee
4. Stewartstown
3. Connecticut Lakes State Forest
2. Keene
1. Merrimack River

State Flag, Seal, and Song

New Hampshire's state flag shows the state seal on a blue background. The seal is surrounded by laurel leaves—a traditional symbol of victory—and nine stars, showing that New Hampshire is the ninth state.

The state seal shows the frigate *Raleigh*—built in Portsmouth in 1776 for the new American navy—with a granite boulder in front and the rising sun behind. This scene is circled by laurel wreaths, the words "Seal of the State of New Hampshire," and the date 1776.

The state legislature adopted "Old New Hampshire" as the official state song in 1949. John Franklin Holmes wrote the lyrics and Maurice Hoffmann wrote the music in 1926. Hoffman played the organ for Manchester's Franklin Street Congregational Church. By 1977, the legislature added eight honorary state songs. The lyrics of "Old New Hampshire" are available at: **www.50states.com/songs/newhamp.htm**.

Glossary

advanced manufacturing Using new technology and other scientific discoveries in the production of goods.

defunct No longer working, operating, or in existence; often used to describe companies or services that go out of business.

echolocation The process of sending out sound waves to locate objects; used by animals such as bats and dolphins.

habitat loss The damage or destruction of an animal's natural home, such as the forest or ocean.

longhouse A type of home, longhouses are large structures made of wood and covered by tree bark.

opaque A quality of something you can't see through, or something that is not transparent, meaning light does not pass through it.

Petits Canadas From the French words for "small Canadas," these are communities in the United States where large numbers of French Canadians live.

precipitation Rain, snow, sleet, or hail that falls from the sky.

predicament A difficult situation, often requiring the participants to make a tough choice.

primary election The first stage of an election in which candidates are chosen by each political party to run for office.

soil erosion A process that moves soil from one location to another by running water, ice, or blowing wind.

treaty A formal agreement between two or more countries, often at the conclusion of war. The Treaty of Portsmouth was signed in New Hampshire at the end of the Russo-Japanese War.

wigwam A dome-shaped hut with a wooden frame that is covered with animal skin or tree bark.

More About New Hampshire

BOOKS

Auden, Scott. *Voices of Colonial America: New Hampshire 1603–1776*. Washington, DC: National Geographic Children's Books, 2007.

Cunningham, Kevin. *The New Hampshire Colony*. New York: Scholastic, 2011.

DiConsiglio, John. *Franklin Pierce: America's 14th President*. Danbury, CT: Children's Press, 2004.

Harris, Marie. *G is for Granite: A New Hampshire Alphabet*. Ann Arbor, MI: Sleeping Bear Press, 2002.

WEBSITES

New Hampshire State Government: Just for Kids page
www.nh.gov/nhfacts

New Hampshire Student Resource Guide
www.visitnh.gov/student/funfacts.html

New Hampshire Tourism: Family Activities
www.visit-newhampshire.com/state/family-activities

ABOUT THE AUTHORS

Kerry Jones Waring is a writer, editor, and communications professional. She lives in Buffalo, New York, with her husband and son, and loves to visit the beaches of New Hampshire.

Terry Allan Hicks is a regular contributor to Cavendish Square Publishing. He lives with his wife and three sons in Connecticut.

William McGeveran is the former editorial director at World Almanac Books who now works as a freelance editor and writer.

Index

Page numbers in **boldface** are illustrations. Entries in **boldface** are glossary terms.

advanced manufacturing, 69
agriculture, 26, 65
    See also farming
American Revolution,
    28–29, 31–32, 43, 47, 52
animals, 18–21, 26–27, 73
area, 7–8
Atlantic Ocean, 8, 29, 34,
    68, 75

birds, 4, 18–20

capital, *See* Concord
cities, *See* Concord;
    Manchester; Nashua
climate, 7, 16–17
colleges and universities,
    28–29,
Concord, 8, 16–17, 29,
    34, 51

defunct, 34

echolocation, 20
economy, 40–42, 65–66,
    69, 72

factories, 8, 34, 36–37, 40,
    45, 47
farming, 23, 27, 31, 65, 68
Frost, Robert, 29, 47–48, 53

geography, 8–9
government, 7, 19, 26, 29,
    31–32, 40, 43, 57–61
governor, 4, 28, 58–60,
    62–63, 73
granite, 5, 7–8, 65
Great Depression, 38–39

habitat loss, 21

laws, 31–33, 58–60, 63
longhouse, 27

Manchester, 8, 34, 37, **38**,
    39, 43, 47, 51, 61, 66, 68
manufacturing, 31, 34, 36–37,
    39–40, 42, 65–66, 69, 72

mountains,
    Cannon Mountain,
        13–14, 49
    Mount Monadnock, 8,
        9, **9**
    Mount Washington,
        12–13, 15–16,
        39–40, 42, 67, 75
    White Mountains,
        8–9, 13, 16, 37, 40,
        71, 73

Nashua, 8, 17, 34, 47, 51, 61
native, 29, 31, 41, 46, 53, 62
Native Americans, 4, 23–26,
    28, 30–31, 45, 47

Old Man of the Mountain,
    13, **13**, 43
opaque, 70

Petits Canadas, 46
politics and politicians,
    7, 33, 42, 57, 60,
    62–63
precipitation, 12

Index

predicament, 32
primary election, 7, 42

Revolutionary War, *See*
American Revolution
rivers, 16, 73
Connecticut River, 16,
28, 55, 68

Merrimack River, 8, 16,
25, 34, **38**, 68
Piscataqua River, 8, 16,
25, 43, 55

settlers, 4, 8, 23–26, 31, 33
slavery, 32–33, 36, 45, 47
soil erosion, 21

technology, 41–42, 51,
66–69, 71
textiles, 34, 37–40, 65–66
treaty, 28, 38

Wentworth, Benning, 4, 28, **28**
wigwam, 27, **27**
World Wars I and II, 38–40